**Nature Crafts
for Children**

Also by Wendy L. Zhorne
Children's Craft Ideas

Nature Crafts for Children

Wendy L. Zhorne

Paul Stoub, Illustrator

Baker Books

A Division of Baker Book House Co
Grand Rapids, Michigan 49516

©1996 by Wendy L. Zhorne

Published by Baker Books
a division of Baker Book House Company
P.O. Box 6287, Grand Rapids, MI 49516-6287

Printed in the United States of America

ISBN 0-8010-5266-1

Dedicated to my precious daughter, **Sophia Rose Zhorne**
Her life has caused a rose to blossom in a desert of pain

Contents

Projects for
New Testament Stories

Acknowledgments

I would like to thank my grandfather, Alexander Rudolph Keller, great-grandson of the royal family of von Kellers from Berlin. His wit, charm, consistent love, and many helpful suggestions for this book made its creation a family project. No, Gramps, you still don't get a cut on the royalties.

To my daddy, Larry Keller, who spent many hours doing crafts with me as a little girl, from string art to plastic flowers. Thanks, Daddy.

My deep admiration and respect to my editor, Betty De Vries, whose consistent enthusiasm for my ideas never ceases to astonish me. I know her as a fine editor and a delightful woman—a true blessing to work with.

And finally to my publisher, Richard Baker, a man whose reputation within Christian publishing is a joy to behold, and whose interactions with me have left me with a sense of his genuineness, business savvy, and determination.

Basic Supply List

Glue
Scissors
Crayons
Construction paper
Tape
Staplers
Acrylic or tempera paint
Brushes
Paint shirts or smocks
Toothpicks
Foil wrapping paper
Crepe and tissue paper
Shellac or varnish
Containers for paint or glue
Newspaper

Familiarize yourself with a project by doing a sample before you present it to the children.

Projects for Old Testament Stories

1

The Creation of Plants

Miniature Growing Plot

Genesis 1:11

Per Child Supplies

12 different seeds, labeled
Half an egg carton (bottom or top)
Potting soil

For older children:
Toothpicks
Paper triangles (postage stamp size)

Teacher Supplies

Measuring cup for potting soil

Instructions

1. Fill each egg cup with potting soil.
2. Write name of plant on each paper triangle, or draw a picture (for example, ear of corn). Skewer with toothpick or attach with tape. Poke into the hole with each seed when it is planted.
3. Plant seeds. Sprinkle lightly with water.

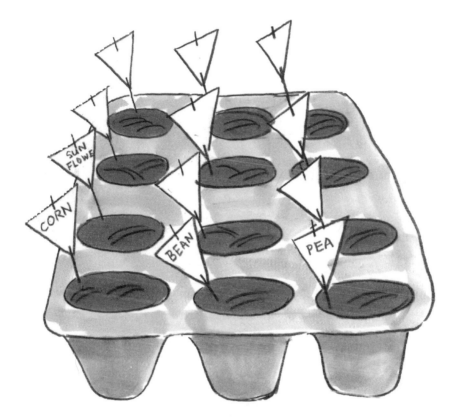

2

Plants Yielding Seed

Seed-Mosaic Boxes

Genesis 1:12

Per Child Supplies

Small box with lid
Collection of seeds (mustard, sunflower, bean, pea, corn, etc.)
Acrylic or tempera paint
Black crayon or pen
Piece of lightweight cardboard
Glue

Instructions

1. Paint all of box except for lid in bright, geometric pattern. While paint is drying, use black pen or crayon to mark out large geometric shapes on box lid. Small children can make simple lines and squares.
2. Carefully apply thin coating of glue to all areas to be covered by one kind of seed (for example, peas). When all areas intended for peas are tacky, sprinkle peas over glue, using piece of cardboard as a shield to other areas. Repeat for all areas/seeds. Lightly press down.
3. If desired, shellac or varnish finished lid when dry.

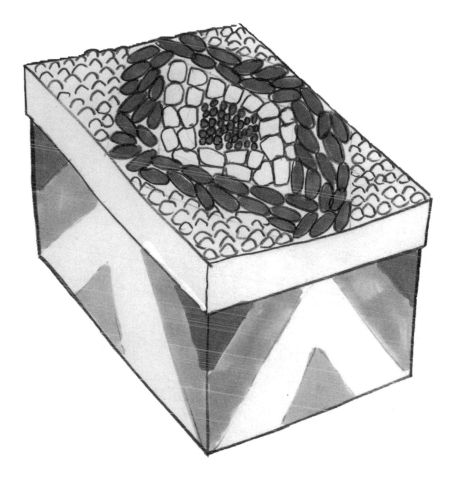

3

Let There Be Light!

Interactive Paper Project

Genesis 1:14

Per Child Supplies

    1 brass brad (the peg with split legs)
    2 sheets blue or black construction paper
    1 sheet yellow construction paper
    1 sheet white construction paper

Teacher Preparation

On half of the dark sheets, draw waves along the middle with white chalk, leaving 2-inch margins on either side. Above the waves, draw an enormous sun with wavy rays.

Punch a hole in the middle of each picture just below the middle of the waves, and in the other three sheets of paper lengthwise just below center.

Instructions

1. Have the children cut the *center* of the picture out—waves, sun, and sun rays. Make sure the margins are not cut!
2. Cut the yellow paper into a large circle, paring not more than 2 inches from either end. Matching the holes, glue a semicircle of white paper over the yellow to form a half-white, half-yellow circle with a hole in the center.
3. Sandwich the circle between the two sheets of dark paper, with the yellow/white side facing the back of the cut (relief) picture.

When the yellow-paper sun is up, the water is illuminated by sunlight. Twist the circle and the moon is on the water.

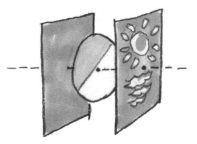

4

The Creation of Birds

Dress-Up Costume

Genesis 1:20

Per Child Supplies

Large rubber band or yarn
Long piece of scrap cloth (about 25 x 4 inches)
Numerous feathers (turkey, chicken, or artificial)
Yellow construction paper
2 large, flimsy paper plates

Teacher Supplies

Hole punch

Teacher Preparation

For beak: Roll construction paper into cone and staple or tape. Punch a hole in each side. Trim. Cut rubber band and tie one end to each side (or use yarn and tie behind head).

For tail: Staple a paper plate to the center of length of cloth.

For headpiece: Cut the interior circle of other paper plate except for 4 inches.

Instructions

1. Glue feathers to both plates, one side only.
2. Draw a mouth and nostrils on the beak with a marker.
3. Put beak over face. Put head through paper plate so front sticks up.
4. Fasten tail around waist like a belt.

5

The Creation of Birds

Birdbath

Genesis 1:20

Per Child Supplies

1 1/2 pounds modeling clay (the kind that dries hard)

1 12-inch long stick

Colored stones, pebbles, beads, or fake gems

Instructions

1. Mold about 1 pound of clay around stick to form 11-inch high self-standing pedestal for birdbath. One inch of stick should protrude.
2. Form basin with remaining clay, saving a few ounces.
3. Press basin down on center of stick. Use last bit of clay to seal the hole, completely covering the stick.
4. Press stones, beads, etc. into the bath to decorate. Allow to dry.

6

The Creation of Birds

Artificial Birds

Genesis 1:20

Per Child Supplies

1 tiny orange triangle for a beak
4-inch styrofoam ball
2-inch styrofoam ball
Orange- or rust-colored pipe cleaners
Real turkey or chicken feathers
2 wiggly craft eyes
Nesting material (sea grass, hay, etc.)
Strawberry pint basket

Instructions

1. Paste feathers to balls. Cover completely. Use moderate glue, or tacky glue.
2. Form feet from pipe cleaners and poke into styrofoam body.
3. Glue on eyes and beak.
4. Make nest in strawberry basket with nesting materials.
5. Put bird in nest.

Ages 9–12

7

The Creation of Sea Creatures

Aquarium

Genesis 1:21

Per Child Supplies

1 styrofoam meat packing container
Blue plastic wrap
4 Popsicle sticks
Large green feathers (optional)
Bright paper for fish bodies
4 or 5 small, light, flexible springs
Small piece of coral
Twist tie
Sand

Instructions

1. Cut out and decorate fish (four or five not more than 2 inches in length). Glue fish to springs.
2. Turn over styrofoam platform so it is rim down. Glue lightly and sprinkle with sand. Affix coral with twist tie. Insert green feathers standing up to form aquarium plants.
3. Poke springs through foam so the fish still wiggle but won't fall off.
4. Insert a Popsicle stick into each corner of platform. Wrap exterior with plastic wrap and tape in place.

8

The Creation of Animals

Stone and Burr Creatures

Genesis 1:24

Per Child Supplies

Selection of all sizes of wiggly craft eyes
Cotton balls for wool coats
1/8-inch strips of brown leather, yarn, or fabric for tails
Black beads for noses
Snippets of red and yellow paper for tongues and beaks
Assortment of pinecones, large burrs, smooth stones
Assorted construction paper for elephant ears, frog feet, etc.

Instructions

Make animals! This is a very creative, low preparation craft. The kids do it themselves.

God Planted a Garden Called Eden

Three-Dimensional Garden

Genesis 2:8

Per Child Supplies

> 2 9-inch pieces of white coated wire (thin, malleable)
> White construction paper
> Small 1/2-inch card
> 8-inch cardboard disk or square, painted green
> Assorted fresh greenery
> Dried or fresh flowers
> Small vines

Instructions

1. For the lattice, cut two strips of white paper 10 x 3 inches and nine pieces 6 1/2 x 2 1/2 inches. Glue together to make lattice.
2. Poke two pieces of wire through cardboard, 3 inches apart, spearing the tabs of one end of the lattice when inserted. Twist into knots or tie together.
3. Bend the wires with the lattice over to form a garden arch. Repeat step 2.
4. Cover the ground of the garden (the cardboard disk) with greenery. If using vines, twist them through the lattice.
5. Write the words "The Garden of Eden" on the 1/2-inch card, and hang it from the lattice arch.

10

Tree of Good and Evil

Tree with Two Sides

Genesis 2:9

Per Child Supplies

1 large, rectangular piece of sturdy bark
2 green treetop shapes, from construction paper
Small flowers (paper, dried, or real)

Instructions

1. Draw a mean or sad face on one of the treetops.
2. Draw a happy face with flowers on the other treetop.
3. Glue one treetop to each side of the bark trunk.

11

The River of Pishon

Miniature River and Landscape

Genesis 2:11

Per Child Supplies

8 1/2 x 11 inch piece of cardboard
Green or beige construction paper
Sand
Varied foliage, kale, or fresh grass clippings, small twigs
Blue florists' foil (diagonal strip at least 10 x 3 inches)

Instructions

1. Glue blue foil to cardboard diagonally and trim ends.
2. Tear the green or beige paper diagonally by hand so each piece is jagged and frayed. Glue a piece to form the banks of the foil river.
3. Spread a thin layer of glue all over the banks of the river and sprinkle with sand. Press down gently and shake off excess.
4. Glue on or staple foliage.

12

Bone of My Bone

Anniversary Gift

Genesis 2:23

Per Child Supplies

Large bone-shaped dog biscuit

Small container of sand

1/2 cup prepared plaster of paris

Metal fingernail file or piece of sandpaper

Gold string or ribbon

3 x 3 inch square paper with calligraphy imprint of Scripture

4 x 8 inch piece of construction paper, any color

Instructions

1. Moisten the sand so it packs firmly. Impress the bone into the sand and then remove. Pour in plaster and let harden.
2. Remove plaster bone and shake off excess sand. File or sand to desired appearance.
3. Fold paper in half lengthwise to form 4 x 4 inch card. Write "Happy Anniversary" on the front. Glue Scripture inside. Affix with ribbon to bone.

13

The Evil Serpent

Toy

Genesis 3:1

Per Child Supplies

6 empty wooden or plastic thread spools, or 6 corks with centers hollowed out

Snippets of glitter, stickers, yarn, brightly colored shapes, wallpaper, etc.

Markers (if using wooden spools)

2 wiggly craft eyes or 2 small pieces of green foil

Length of red yarn

Plastic yarn needle

Instructions

1. Tie a large knot in one end of the yarn and string all spools together. Seal with another knot, and fray the knot to form a tongue. Leave some slack.
2. Decorate snake with snippets and markers. Add eyes.

14

Adam and Evening Wear

Clothing of Leaves

Genesis 3:7

Per Child Supplies

Access to many large, fresh leaves
2 1-yard pieces of rope
10–20 twist ties

Instructions

1. Collect a dozen or more leaves of various shapes.
2. Tie the ends of one piece of rope together to form a circle. Affix leaves to rope with twist ties. Put rope around neck.
3. Tie other rope around waist. Affix leaves to long, loose ends of belt rope. Tie in a bow behind the back.

15

The Brothers' Offerings

Fruit Bowl

Genesis 4:3

Per Child Supplies

8-inch wooden circle of 1/2-inch plywood with six 3/8-inch holes bored almost all the way through perimeter

Wood glue

6 lengths of sturdy twigs, not exceeding 3/8 inch in diameter

Large quantity of supple vines, such as fresh grape or ivy, as long as possible (use jute if no vines are available)

Twist ties

Instructions

1. Break all twigs to approximately equal lengths. Poke into holes and fill cracks with glue.
2. Remove all foliage from vines. If they have begun to stiffen, soak in a tub of hot water and salt for a half hour or so.
3. Weave the vines in and out around the twigs in the basket, loosely enclosing the twigs and tucking the ends in when appropriate to begin a new vine (affix with twist ties until dried in place). With rope, follow the same pattern but do not tuck in ends until finished.
4. Allow glue and vines to dry before use. Always lift from the bottom.

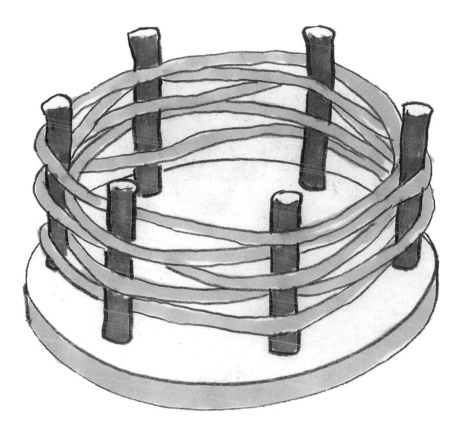

16

The Legacy of Tubal-Cain

Metalwork Sculpture

Genesis 4:22

Per Child Supplies

Thin square of malleable copper or artist-weight aluminum
Orangewood cuticle stick or craft stick and blunt pencil
Smooth stone
Access to engravings (cemetery stones or stone bas-relief) or thick
piece of felt
Piece of mounting wood larger than the metal (can be painted or stained)
4 nails

Instructions

1. If using engravings, attach metal to engraving with masking tape. Carefully rub over entire piece with stone, detailing with orangewood stick, until the shape or inscription becomes visible.
2. If not using engravings, place metal over felt on hard surface. Draw a design on the metal, using the blunt end of the orangewood stick as well as the stone and other sturdy objects (scissor handles, small pebbles, etc.) to form a design.
3. When the etching is complete, mount on board using nails.

Comments

Certain chemicals will stain a copper sheet interesting colors. A number of them are nontoxic and would add dimension to this project for older children. Consult your local art supply dealer.

17

The Ark of Noah

3-D Sculpture

Genesis 6:14

Per Child Supplies

Bath-size bar of soap
Butter knife
Sharpened pencils
Fork

Instructions

1. Using a completed project as an example, show a bar of soap that has been carved into the shape of a ship. (Adults might find an X-Acto knife speedier.) Use plenty of detail. The completed project might have a cabin above a vast hull, cut lengthwise on the soap for added height.
2. Have the children carve a ship from the soap using a butter knife. Pick out windows using a sharp pencil. The wood grain on the sides is accomplished by raking the sides with a fork.
3. After the project is complete either dip quickly into warm water to smooth out the rough edges or rub over it with a cloth dipped in warm water. (Test the soap brand beforehand. The softer the soap, the cooler the water must be to prevent melting.)

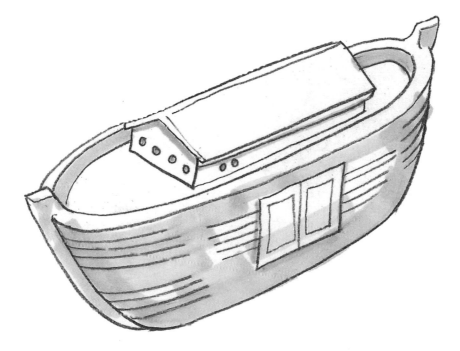

18

Every Creeping Thing

Jumping Spiders

Genesis 7:14

Per Child Supplies

6 black pipe cleaners (the chenille kind)
2 small, wiggly craft eyes
Length of elastic string

Instructions

1. Bend four pipe cleaners in half and bind together once with fifth piece. Separating each leg, weave the fifth cleaner around and between the spider's legs until there are eight legs, four per side.
2. Tie one end of the elastic string to the spider's midsection. Tie a loop in the other end.
3. Use the remaining pipe cleaner to flesh out the body and cover the knotted string. Glue on eyes.

19

God's Bow in the Clouds

Multicolored Twig Bow

Genesis 9:13

Per Child Supplies

1 yard each of 3 different rainbow-colored pieces of yarn

Bendable twig at least 2 1/2 feet long

6 construction-paper triangles in rainbow colors, each with a 1-inch base

6 6-inch lengths of old twig, sliced slightly if necessary to split ends

Instructions

1. Braid the three pieces of yarn together. (Knot three pieces together and then attach knot to the edge of a desk with masking tape for younger children.)
2. Tie one end of the braid to the longer twig. Then bending the bow slightly, tie other end.
3. To make arrows, write a Christian value on each triangle with bright crayon. If the twigs are old, the tips can be split 1/2 inch or so with a fingernail. Otherwise, slice with a knife or thin-bladed saw. Insert paper triangle into slit. Glue if necessary.

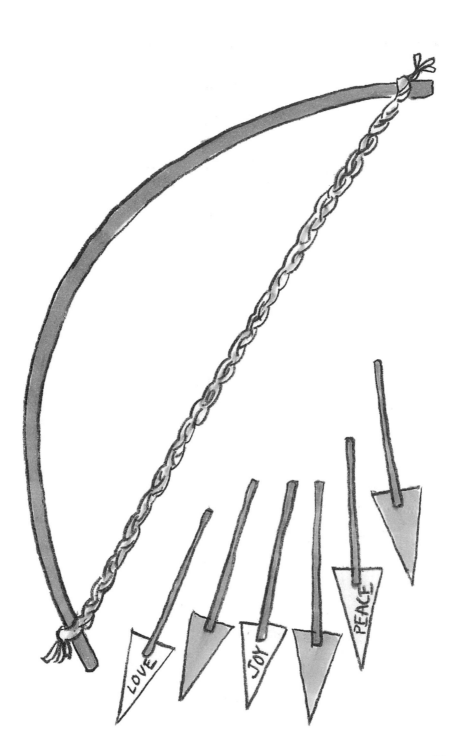

20

God Is a Shield to Abram

Shield

Genesis 15:1

Per Child Supplies

2 sticks lashed together to form a cross
Piece of cloth, animal skin, or brown paper sack
Tailor's chalk
Yarn needle for cloth or skin, stapler for sack
Length of yarn
Thumb tacks (4)

Instructions

1. Place the cloth, skin, or sack on a table. Place the cross frame over the cloth, and trace around with a piece of tailor's chalk leaving a 2-inch margin. Cut out.
2. Using yarn, connect the edges of the cross to form a kite-shaped outline. Attach to ends of sticks with tacks.
3. Fold over the fabric, skin, or paper margin. String the yarn through the needle and slip stitch to frame. Staples may be used for paper.

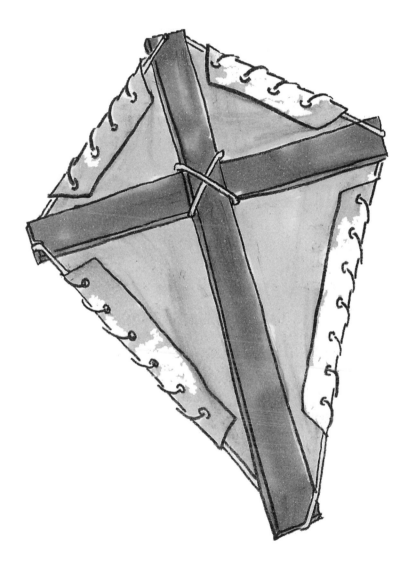

21

A Skin of Water for Hagar

Water Container/Flower Vase

Genesis 21:14

Per Child Supplies

Interestingly shaped empty glass bottle (wine or juice bottles work great)
Roll of masking tape
Cordovan-colored shoe polish
Small cotton rag

Instructions

1. Remove any label from the bottle and wash thoroughly.
2. Tear pieces of masking tape so that all edges are ragged. Smaller pieces look better, but the project completion time is longer. Starting at the bottom of the bottle, apply dime-sized tape pieces, covering the entire bottle and overlapping each piece of tape.
3. Firmly press tape, roll bottle to adhere all bits of tape. Using small rag, wipe bottle lightly with shoe polish.

22

Rebekah's Water Jar

Clay Amphora

Genesis 24:16

Per Child Supplies

Cork
Self-hardening modeling clay (beige or russet colored)
Red tempera paint (optional)

Instructions

1. Using the cork as a size guide for the neck opening, fashion a clay amphora (elongated, pointed-bottom jar used for carrying water).
2. Remove cork and allow to dry. Neck will shrink slightly, so make slightly larger than cork when wet or the cork will have to be whittled to fit. When dry, paint with red designs or Hebrew characters.

23

Ancient Jewels

Handmade Jewelry

Genesis 24:22

Per Child Supplies

Pretty stones or beads, especially shiny ones
1 yard of malleable wire (coated electrical wire works well)
Varnish (optional)

Instructions

1. If so desired, or if the only rocks available aren't particularly attractive, dip in varnish and allow to dry.
2. Leaving a 6-inch lead, begin wrapping first stone in wire. Some rocks can be secured by wrapping around twice; others must be secured by going around horizontally, then vertically like a gift package.
3. Without cutting wire, move on to second rock, etc., until all rocks or wire have been used. Form a necklace by using the 6-inch lead to join ends.
4. Form a hook and eye closure.

Comments

Sometimes gemologists or rock shops carry quantities of cheap rocks like quartz. Gravel companies might also have things of interest. This project can also be done with bark chips.

24

Sands of the Seashore

Sand Art

Genesis 32:12

Per Child Supplies

1 small glass jar (baby food size)
Sand in three shades of blue (purchase or dye with food coloring)
1/4 of an egg carton
Small seashell
Toothpicks and Popsicle sticks
Teaspoon

Instructions

1. Pour each color of sand into part of egg carton for easy access. With teaspoon, layer sand into jar unevenly, starting with the darkest blue on the bottom.
2. Create mounds by piling sand against the jar's interior, and repeat with other colors until all three colors have been used. Jar should be three-quarters full.
3. With a toothpick and Popsicle stick, carefully press down the sand to form a wavelike pattern visible from the outside of the jar. Use caution and patience. When project is satisfactory, top with sea shell.

Comments

Sand may be permanently hardened into this pattern by slowly adding thinned varnish or shellac using shell to dispel the displacement force of varnish. Or use a turkey baster, *slowly* dropping varnish in.

25

The Cupbearer's Dream

Decorated Glass

Genesis 40:13

Per Child Supplies

1 cheap wine glass (for younger kids, a plastic wine glass works great)
Assortment of fabric paints
Small craft jewels or flat-backed rhinestone studs
Gold paint (optional)

Instructions

1. Using a clean, dry glass, paint any decoration on the glass with a light application of fabric paint.
2. Apply beads, jewels, or rhinestones with a dab of fabric paint, but not so much that it runs off. Stand on rim to dry overnight.
3. When dry, burnish with rag dipped in gold paint.

26

Seven Fat Cows

Creamer

Genesis 41:2

Per Child Supplies

1/2 pound of white, self-hardening, nontoxic clay
Black and white oil paint
2 small, fake bear claws or elephant tusks not more than 1 inch long
2 wiggly craft eyes

Instructions

1. Form a hollow cow body with two-thirds of the clay, about the size of three-fourths of a toilet paper tube, sealed at either end and open in the center.
2. Form cow-shaped legs and head, and score body on attachment points to help bond limbs securely to body. Press eyes and horns (claws or tusks) into head.
3. Form handle by making a sturdy tail of clay and attaching securely by scoring deeply and using a little water.
4. Allow to dry. Paint to look like a cow.

Comments

The cow's paint will last through a few washings. To ensure longevity, it may be glazed and fired, but be certain to use real clay if you plan on this procedure.

27

Seven Withered Ears

Model

Genesis 41:23

Per Child Supplies

Yellow corn cereal (small, football-shaped pieces)
Craft stick or Popsicle stick
2 pieces of freshly shucked corn husk
Brown yarn or twine

Instructions

1. Glue corn cereal to Popsicle stick in rows, using minimal amount of glue.
2. Cover entire stick with husks and secure with yarn or twine.

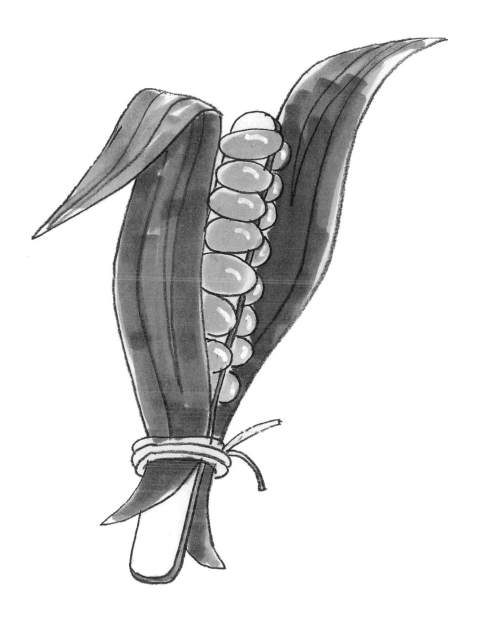

28

The Burning Bush

Candle

Exodus 3:2

Per Child Supplies

Red, yellow, and orange crayons

Melted paraffin wax

Empty, clean, juice concentrate cylinder with one end removed

2-inch black, coated electrical wire

6-inch length of cotton wick or twine

Instructions

1. Shape wire into a long tree shape with many branches. Insert entirely into juice can.
2. Remove labels from crayons and mix into hot paraffin wax. Silver and gold can be added for sparkly effect. Mix thoroughly.
3. Tape one end of wick to a pencil. Lay pencil over juice can, making sure that wick is centered and touches the bottom of can. Pour hot wax into can and allow to cool slightly.
4. When the wax is warm but not hot (a few hours), peel off juice can and pick out the wire branches so they stick out of the candle.

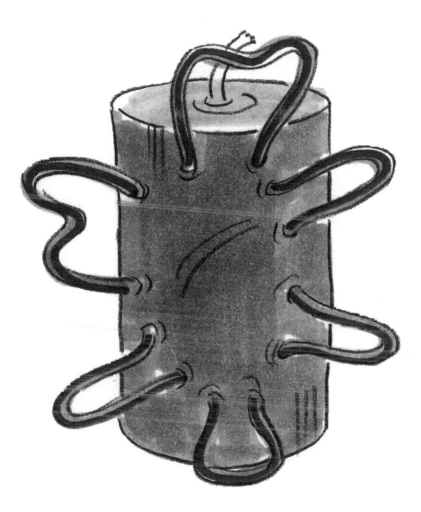

29

The Burning Bush

Model

Exodus 3:2

Per Child Supplies

1 twiggy branch
A few sheets of aluminum foil
Orange, yellow, and red finger or tempera paint

Instructions

1. Paint entire surface of sheets of foil. When partially dry (use a blow-dryer for speed), wrap all but one sheet of foil around branch, poking tips of twigs through as necessary.
2. Wrap last sheet of foil around the base of twig for support.

30

Plague of Insects

Toy

Exodus 8:24

Per Child Supplies

18-inch long dowel or stick
Yarn
Piece of 1/2-inch foam rubber cut according to template
Markers or tempera paint
2 wiggly craft eyes

Instructions

1. Paint pieces of foam rubber with markers or paint.
2. Attach to stick with yarn. Glue on eyes.
3. Paint with vivid colors.

Comments

Wings should be loose so that when the stick is wiggled they float up and down slightly.

31

The Ten Commandments

Plaque

Exodus 20

Per Child Supplies

Selection of alphabet noodles dyed blue or red (soak in dye and then dry)

Two thin pieces of self-drying clay

A copy of the Ten Commandments

Length of yarn

Instructions

1. Form clay into one piece, shaped like two tablets joined together. Score down center for effect.
2. Press noodles into clay to spell out one or two of the Ten Commandments.
3. Poke a hole through plaque near the top for hanging on a nail. Allow to dry. If desired, coat with glossy varnish when clay is dry.

32

No Other Gods before Me

Wall Hanging

Exodus 20:3

Per Child Supplies

1 or 2 leaves with pronounced venation
Petroleum jelly
Thin saucer or pie tin
Prepared liquid plaster of paris
Large paper clip
Calligraphy copy of commandment
Shellac or mixture of 2/3 glue, 1/3 water
Paint

Instructions

1. Heavily grease bowl or pie tin. Press leaves venation side up into the bottom. Overlap is okay.
2. Pour in plaster mix and lay paper clip, bent slightly open, in the middle to form a hanger.
3. When dry, remove from bowl, take off leaves, and paint. Place copy of commandment over the front, and shellac or glue-varnish over entire project.

33

The Temple Curtains

Weaving

Exodus 26

Per Child Supplies

> 2 2-foot long branches not more than 1 inch in diameter (bent is fine)
> Skein of red or purple yarn
> Skein of interesting, fluffy gold or silver yarn, or 2-inch wide ribbon (about 2 yards)
> Short, fat, bumpy stick
> Wire coat hanger
> Twist ties

Instructions

1. Fasten one branch to the coat hanger along the horizontal bar using twist ties. This is only to hold the project in place while it is being completed. Hanger and ties will be discarded later.
2. Hang coat hanger about the height of a doorknob or off the edge of a desk or table. Place other branch directly on floor below. Using red or purple yarn, wrap the two together, maintaining the floor-to-doorknob distance and leaving 2-inch margins on both ends of sticks. Loop over and over until not fewer than 24 loops have been made.
3. Tie one end of gold or silver yarn or ribbon to short, fat, bumpy stick. Using the stick to guide, weave from the bottom over one, under one, over one, under one, capturing each horizontal thread between the two branches. Without cutting yarn or ribbon, repeat until the entire floor-to-top-branch space has been filled. (Some gaps are to be expected.) Firmly tie each end of the yarn or ribbon to the branch.
4. Affirm that project is secured. Remove ties and use a wire cutter to remove wire hanger or leave it as a hanger for the project.

34

The High Priest's Breastplate

Jewelry

Exodus 39:8

Per Child Supplies

4 notched craft sticks
12 small craft jewels, buttons, or snips of dime-sized colored foil
Yarn
Paint, crayons, or markers

Instructions

1. Paint or color the sticks.
2. Using an 18-inch piece of yarn, tie the craft sticks parallel to one another. Form a necklace with sticks (about 1/2 inch apart) on chest. Rest of yarn goes around neck and can be adjusted.
3. Then glue three different colored stones or jewels on each stick.

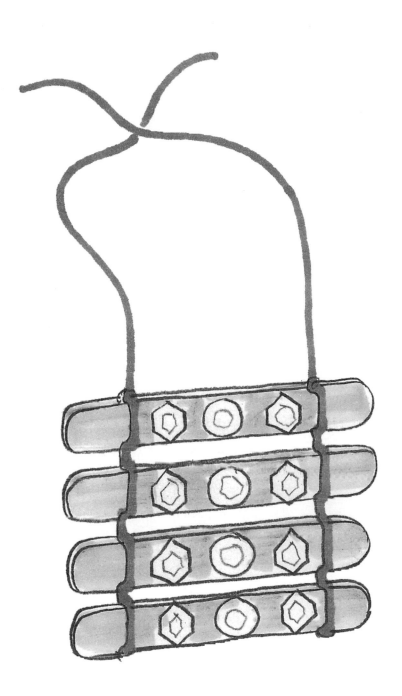

35

The Settlement along the Jordan

Miniature Landscape

Deuteronomy 3:20

Per Child Supplies

Selection of small twigs and foliage
Pebbles
Box top with at least 1/2-inch lip
Blue and green construction paper
Yarn
Modeling clay
Small swatches of brightly patterned fabric

Instructions

1. Glue green paper inside the box lid. Tear blue paper diagonally and glue over green to form a river.
2. Alongside the riverbank, form tents, glue pebbles and small foliage, and make a campfire with clay and tiny twigs.
3. To form tents: Cut piece of fabric in elongated wedge shape. Hold three twigs together and wrap fabric around like a teepee. Secure with bit of yarn. Use clay to affix tent legs to box.
4. To make campfire: Form small flame shapes with red clay. Press onto small bundle of twigs to form fire.

36

Samson's Fox Fire

Candleholder

Judges 15:4

Per Child Supplies

Modeling clay
Paint
Short brown or red taper (3 inches)
2 small, wiggly craft eyes
Russet and white paint
Small, black bead for nose

Instructions

1. Mold a fox-shaped body from the clay. Make the fox seem to be sitting down on his haunches. Where the tail would be, mold a large crescent with a hollow center big enough for the candle base. Create markings for fun by etching clay with a fork. Press in eyes and nose. Allow to dry.
2. Paint the fox with a white underbelly and the rest russet, brown, or red. Insert candle.

37

The Joyous Tambourines

Musical Toy

1 Samuel 18:6

Per Child Supplies

Supple vines, like grape or morning glory, at least 4 feet long
6 or more small jingle bells
Carpet thread
Twist ties

Instructions

1. Remove all leaves and twigs from vines. Starting at thickest end, weave vine into itself to form a circle no bigger than a pie plate. Close end with twist tie or tuck into self so it is secure.
2. Use carpet thread (or twist ties for younger children) to attach bells evenly around perimeter of vine wreath. Will remain useful even after it dries in about three weeks.

38

Saul's Spear

Toy

1 Samuel 19:10

Per Child Supplies

Sturdy, straight, blunt stick about 8 inches long
Yarn
Brightly colored electrical tape
Construction paper

Instructions

1. Wrap spear with colored electrical tape. If it doesn't adhere well, the stick is dirty. Rub vigorously with a cloth and try again.
2. Cut triangular arrowhead shape from construction paper, leaving an extra piece attached to the base to wrap around the stick. Affix arrowhead to end of stick with yarn.

39

Naaman's Bath

Paper Construction

2 Kings 5

Per Child Supplies

1 pink, brown, or white cutout from template
Brown, dark blue, light blue, and white construction paper
1 paper strip 1 1/2 x 5 inches
6-inch piece of blue yarn
8 1/2 x 11 inch cardboard

Instructions

1. Cut out jumping Naaman, large brown rock, dark blue waves, and white clouds. Glue light blue construction paper to cardboard for background.
2. Glue waves onto bottom of cardboard, leaving 1/2-inch opening for yarn in lower right quadrant about 3 inches from edge. Yarn should be under waves and hanging out either side. Glue large brown rock on right, leaving yarn free.
3. Glue Naaman to yarn at his stomach. On his back attach 1 1/2 x 5 inch paper strip. Glue on clouds, covering but leaving free the paper strip, which when pulled, should bring Naaman back onto the rock. To move him into the water, pull the yarn.

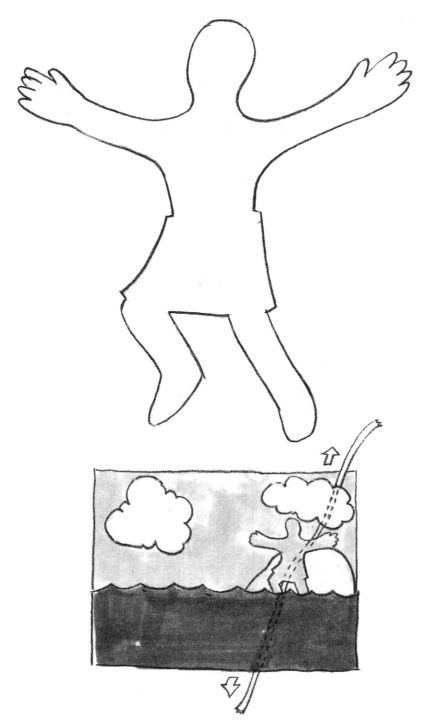

40

Warrior's Rations

Play Dishes

1 Chronicles 12:39

Per Child Supplies

Twigs and short sticks
Self-drying clay
Heart- or triangle-shaped pasta, or bright beads
Twine, jute, or yarn

Instructions

1. To form plate, press and roll clay into plate shape with slight lip. Press pasta or beads in to decorate. Paint when dry if desired.
2. To form utensils, bind three sturdy 1-inch twigs to short stick with twine to form the tines on a rustic fork.
3. For older children, whittle another short stick to form a knife.

Comments

This project can be brushed over lightly with copper paint to create a nice effect when it is dry. However, that does make it toxic.

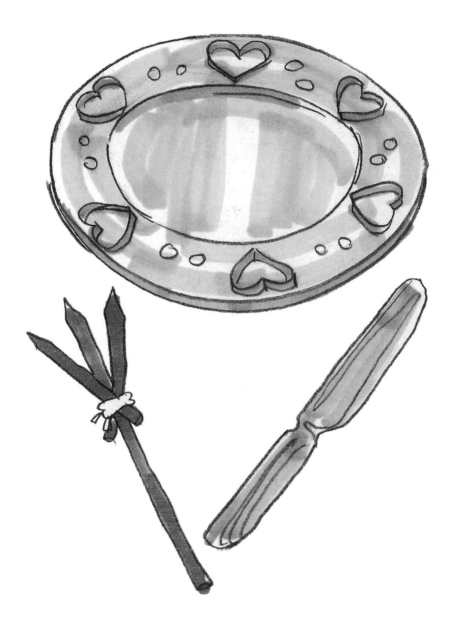

Temple Basins

Decorative Bowls

1 Chronicles 28:17

Per Child Supplies

> 1 1/2 pounds of clay
> Small ceramic bathroom tiles (come in sheets)
> Beads, bits of broken plastic, or buttons
> Small cloth
> Gold paint

Instructions

1. Form clay into bowl shape with thick sides. Press tiles, beads, plastic, or buttons into outside and around inner perimeter of bowl to form creative designs. Possibilities are flowers, birds, fruit, warriors, holy images.
2. Before the clay dries, wipe a small amount of gold paint with cloth all over bowl, inside and out. Take care to wipe excess off tiles and decorative pieces well. Allow to dry.

Reed Boats

Toy

Job 9:26

Per Child Supplies

Small twigs
1-pint milk carton
Twine
Brown clay

Instructions

1. Break all twigs into roughly the same length. Using the carton as a mold, arrange the twigs side by side over the carton to form the hull of an upside-down boat. Bind ends of twigs securely with twine.
2. Daub with clay between the twigs.
3. When dry, turn over and cut side from carton.

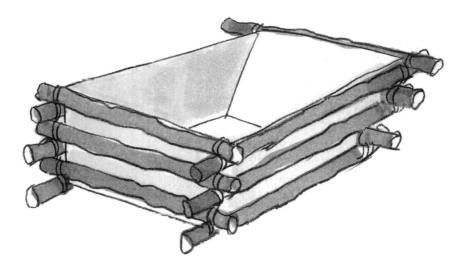

43

I Am but a Worm

Worm Home

Psalm 22:6

Per Child Supplies

2 8 1/2 x 11 inch sheets of sturdy, clear plastic (like Plexiglas) or glass

12-inch piece of wood, 1/2 inch thick, with 2 11-inch grooves cut into it at least 1 inch apart.

2 8 1/2-inch pieces of wood with grooves at least 1 inch apart

2 12-inch pieces of corner trim

Nails and hammer

About 1 cup of soil

Worm

Grass seedlings or small plants

Instructions

1. Lay longest wood down, grooves up. Insert plastic or glass into grooves and mark where it ends. Remove glass. Attach both end pieces at marks, nailing in place. Insert glass down grooves so that it fits snugly.
2. Sprinkle in soil. Add worm and vegetation.
3. Reinforce top by hammering on the two pieces of corner trim, one on either side of the worm tank along the top.

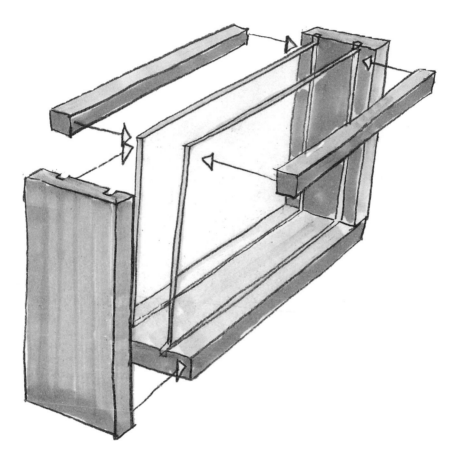

44

The Lord Is My Light

Candleholder

Psalm 27:1

Per Child Supplies

Flat-bottomed pinecone with top third sawn off
Fast-drying clay
Glitter
Votive candle

Instructions

1. Remove one or two rows of "petals" from pinecone. Lightly glue and glitter edges of remaining rows.
2. Affix candle to cone with clay, or drive a headless nail into the center of the cone and press candle down onto it.

45

Banner of Faith

Wall Hanging

Proverbs 3:25

Per Child Supplies

Branch at least 1 foot long
Piece of burlap at least 12 x 8 inches
Yarn needle and yarn
Felt
Scripture printed on paper

Instructions

1. Affix burlap to branch lengthwise with yarn.
2. Cut from felt things that are feared—spiders, monsters, snakes, water, whatever.
3. Glue or sew Scripture and felt shapes onto burlap to form a banner.

Charm Is Deceitful

Plaque

Proverbs 31:30

Per Child Supplies

Dried pressed flowers or leaves
Piece of heavy-weight linen or rag paper
Scripture in calligraphy
Shellac or mixture of 2/3 glue, 1/3 water

Instructions

1. Tear edges of paper to form an attractive shape not more than 6 inches, preferably oval. Punch hole in the top for hanging. Glue on flowers and Scripture.
2. Lightly brush over entire project with glue or shellac, or have it professionally laminated.

Proverbs 31:30

Charm is deceptive and beauty is fleeting; but a woman who fears the Lord is to be praised.

47

Jonah in the Belly

Papier-Mâché Fish with Man Inside

Jonah

Per Child Supplies

Small, inflated balloon	Clothespin
Bit of fabric	Yarn
Strips of newspaper	Mixture of 2/3 glue, 1/3 water
Paint	2 large, wiggly craft eyes
Markers	Crepe paper

Piece of clear plastic the size of credit card

Small red rubber band or 1 1/2 inches of yarn

Instructions

1. Using inflated balloon as a form for the fish's body, lay strips of newspaper moistened in glue mixture around the body, leaving a 1/2-inch space around the knot of the balloon. Leave a gap the size of a credit card and apply plastic piece. Continue applying layers of newspaper until three or four layers have been put in place. Leave the plastic uncovered but attached. This will form a window into the fish's belly.
2. Allow to dry overnight. While drying, paint a face on the clothespin and dress in fabric. Glue on a snippet of yarn for the hair.
3. Puncture and remove balloon. Paint the fish and glue on eyes and red yarn or rubber band to form mouth. Insert Jonah through the hole so he is visible through the plastic and use hot glue or clay to adhere him. Use the crepe paper to fashion a tail. Glue tail into hole to seal.

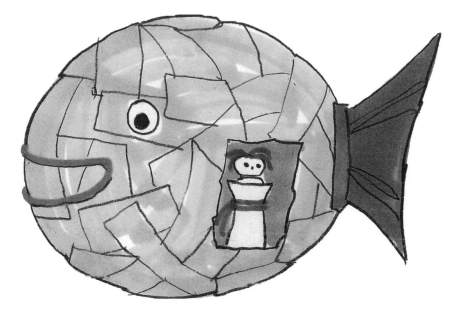

Projects for New
Testament Stories

48

The Magi's Gifts

Decorative Dishes

Matthew 2:11

Per Child Supplies

> 1 white or pale melamine or ceramic dish
> 2 pieces of gold braid for handles
> Small foil stars and crescents
> Pressed flowers or leaves
> Shellac or mixture of 2/3 glue, 1/3 water

Instructions

> 1. Glue stars and flowers or leaves to plate. Cover with shellac or glue to seal.
> 2. Hot glue on pieces of gold braid to form handles.

49

John the Baptist's Clothes

Garment

Matthew 3:4

Per Child Supplies

Approximately 1 1/2 yards of burlap
Yarn
Plastic yarn needle
Felt
3 1-yard pieces of jute

Instructions

1. Cut three pieces from burlap: one long square with notch for neck-line and arm holes and two front panels for either side of garment. Cut various shapes from felt, and glue or sew onto jacket panels.
2. Right sides together, slip stitch shoulder seams then side seams to form a coat. Braid jute together to form a belt.

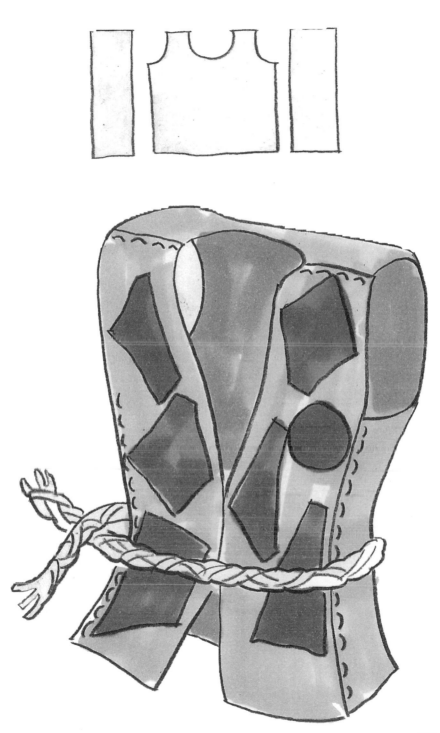

50

The Salt of the Earth

Salt and Pepper Shakers

Matthew 5:13

Per Child Supplies

Nontoxic quick-drying clay
Round toothpick
2 small corks
Paint

Instructions

1. Form clay into two hollow jars like a pinch pot. Start at the bottom and pinch the clay in a circle until it forms a sphere. Leave neck open enough to insert cork firmly. Use bits of flat clay shaped like the continents to apply to the outside. Score and wet slightly to affix.
2. In the side of one pot, poke holes with toothpick in the shape of a cross. In the other, three random holes in a triangle shape.
3. Dry. Then paint to represent the earth.

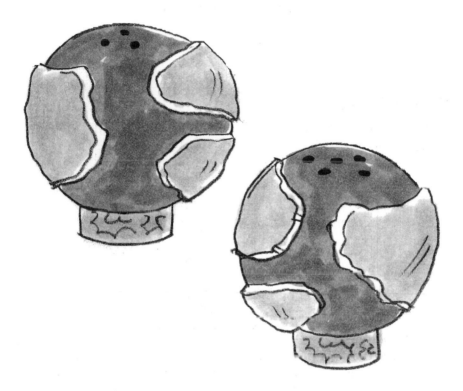

51

Lilies of the Field

Fabric Sculpture

Matthew 6:28

Per Child Supplies

Alene's Tacky Glue (or Fabric glue if Alene's unavailable)
White coated wire
Green and orange fabric
2 yellow pipe cleaners
Red paint
4 pieces thin, green florists' wire
Florists' tape

Instructions

1. Cut fabric using the templates: four green leaves from the longer shape, four orange petals from the shorter shape. With black marker, make dots on orange fabric like a tiger lily.
2. Form coated wire into petal shape following template. Twist to secure. Dip lightly in glue, then immediately press on the orange fabric. Shape naturally. Repeat for each petal. Allow to dry.
3. Lightly dip green wire in tacky glue. Affix to green fabric so that wire forms spine of leaf. Repeat for each leaf. Allow to dry.
4. Cut each yellow pipe cleaner in half. Bend each piece in half and dip tip in red paint. Allow to dry.
5. To assemble, twist petals tightly around yellow pipe cleaners. Add leaves. Wrap stem with florists' tape. (Pull tightly to adhere—it works like a rubber band.)

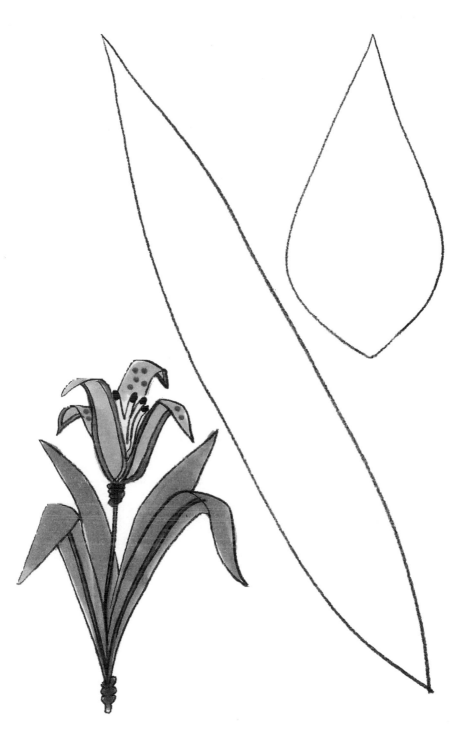

52

Birds Have Their Nests

String Dispenser for Birds

Matthew 8:20

Per Child Supplies

1 empty spool
6 lengths of red or bright green embroidery floss
Piece of paper the size of a label for spool
Piece of yarn for hanging

Instructions

1. Cut out and write Scripture on a piece of paper. Glue to spool where thread was, overlapping slightly.
2. Insert embroidery floss into center of spool, leaving it hanging loose out either end. Tie with yarn into nearby tree.

Comments

The birds will use this string to build their nests. The birds who used it can then be traced because the floss is such a vibrant color. Refillable.

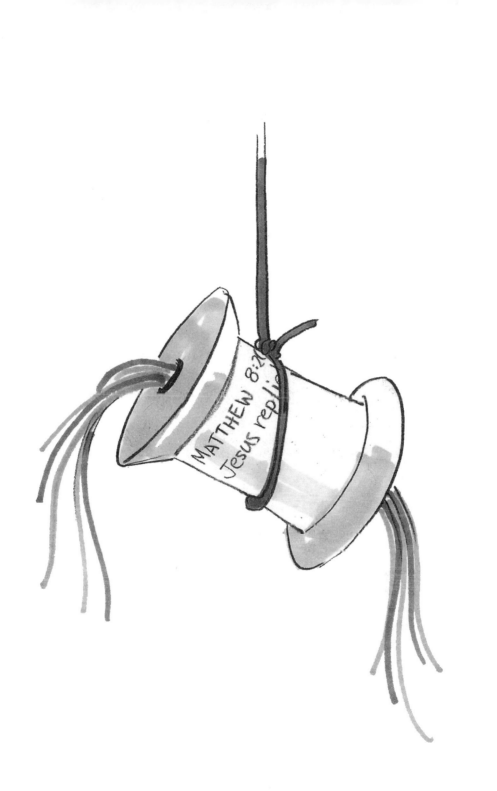

On This Rock Shall I Build My Church

Model

Matthew 16:18

Per Child Supplies

Large, flat rock
1-pint milk carton
Construction paper
Toothpicks for making a steeple (optional)
Small pieces of orange, purple, or yellow tissue paper
Carpet thread

Instructions

1. Cover carton with paper; staple in place.
2. Trace the window cutout from the next page onto black paper. Cut out window panes, making certain not to cut seams. Lay atop tissue paper to size. Cut and glue tissue paper to black paper to form a stained glass window.
3. For small children, glue windows on. For older children, cut holes for windows in the sides of the church, leaving margin to glue window on.
4. Form steeple by lashing toothpicks together and gluing in place. Lightly glue entire structure to rock platform.

54

Faith as a Mustard Seed

Sun Catcher

Matthew 17:20

Per Child Supplies

Mustard seed
Piece of cardboard
Colored construction paper
2 sheets of plastic wrap
Yarn
Tissue paper in bright colors

Instructions

1. Cut cardboard into two diamond or circle shapes about 6 inches in diameter. Cut out center leaving a 2-inch margin. Use as a pattern to cut out two diamonds or circles from colored construction paper.
2. Cut plastic wrap to slightly larger than inner circle or diamond shape. Glue one piece to cardboard. (Glue will not hold yet.) On the cardboard margin around the edge of the plastic wrap, glue pieces of torn tissue paper so that torn edges cover all but the inner, quarter-sized center of frame.
3. Roll mustard seed in glue and place in center. Glue second sheet of plastic wrap to frame, sealing in both tissue paper and seed. Loop yarn and glue to edge to form hanger.
4. Glue the other side of the frame together. Staple if needed. Write Scripture on the perimeter.

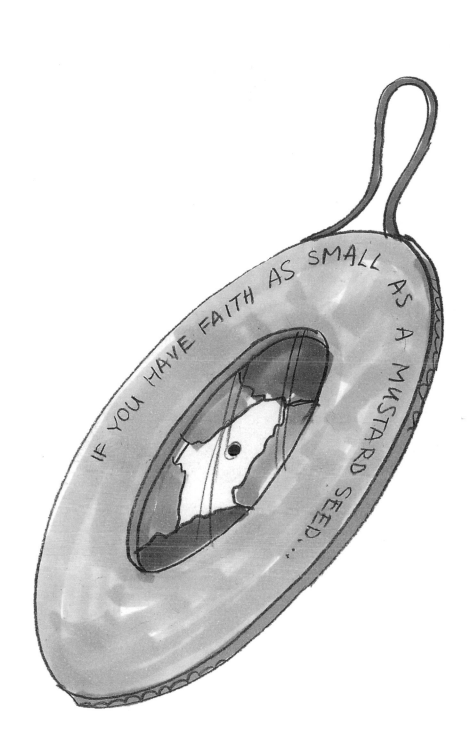

55

Brood of Vipers

Rattlesnake Noisemaker Toy

Matthew 23:33

Per Child Supplies

1 large paper clip
1 small paper clip
1 rubber band
Envelope

Instructions

1. Write on outside of envelope, "CAUTION: BABY RATTLESNAKE INSIDE."
2. Unfold large paper clip. String rubber band across paper clip from end to end like a harp. Bend over the ends to secure. Place small paper clip widthwise in the middle of rubber band. It should look like a letter *E*. Twist small paper clip and when the rubber band is fully wound, carefully place it into the envelope. Hold in place until offering it to someone to look at. When the envelope is opened, the unwinding rubber band beats the small paper clip against the paper and sounds like a rattlesnake.

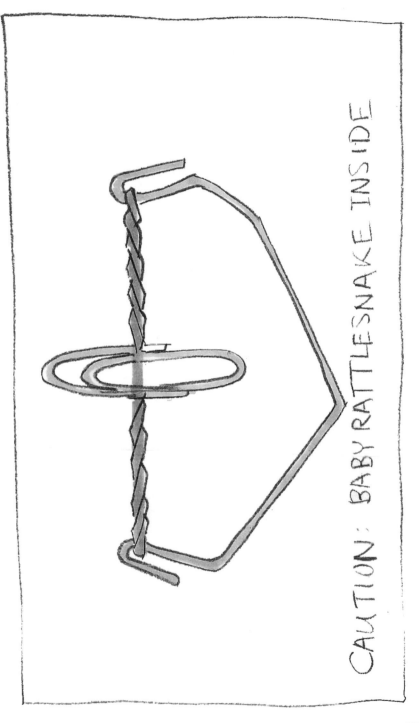

CAUTION: BABY RATTLESNAKE INSIDE

56

A Hen with Her Chicks

Papier-Mâché Sculpture

Matthew 23:37

Per Child Supplies

Balloon
2 blown-empty eggshells
Newspaper strips
Mixture of 2/3 glue, 1/3 water
Paint
Artificial feathers
4 small and 2 large, wiggly craft eyes
Yellow pipe cleaners
Small, felt, diamond-shaped beaks

Instructions

1. For hen: Blow up balloon. Wet strips of newspaper and glue onto balloon, covering entirely. Repeat with eggshells for the chicks. Set aside to dry.
2. Fashion wings from wet newspaper by placing an appropriately sized newspaper wing shape flat on table. Glue feathers 1/4 inch from edge. Glue another wing-shaped piece of newspaper, slightly smaller, overlapping 1/4 inch. Glue on feathers until wing is three or four layers thick.
3. When dry, paint and glue on wings. Pierce hen's body with a pencil and insert two pipe-cleaner feet and beak. Glue feet on chicks. Glue on eyes, beak, and feathers.

57

Perfume for Christ

Potpourri

Matthew 26:7

Per Child Supplies

Collection of dried flowers, seed pods, bark chips, etc.
Small glass jar with lid
Few drops of sandalwood or patchouli oil
Square of gingham, cut with pinking shears
Ribbon or rubber band
Placard with Scripture

Instructions

1. In large, nonmetallic bowl, place all botanical elements. Mix with oil like a salad. Fill jar and close.
2. Place gingham over jar lid. Affix with ribbon or rubber band. Attach small placard.

Comments

Makes a nice gift for elderly folks.

58

Birds Nest in Its Shade

Birdhouse

Mark 4:32

Per Child Supplies

6 x 6 inch cardboard box
2 pieces of scrap composite shingle
Shredded rags
Serrated knife or scissors
Paint
Rope or jute

Instructions

1. Seal box and slice small bird-sized hole in side. Poke rags inside.
2. Paint box like a small house. Paint on windows, welcome sign, etc. Put shingles on roof with staples or nails.
3. Hang in tree by cradling with rope or jute beneath the tip, like a hammock. Use several strands and tie together above the house.

Ages 6 & up

59

Possessed Pigs

Model

Mark 5:12

Per Child Supplies

Self-drying modeling clay
Pink pipe cleaner
Pink paint
Felt pig ears
2 large, wiggly craft eyes

Instructions

1. Mold clay into shape of a pig. Press on felt ears and cover base of ears with clay to secure.
2. Twist pipe cleaner around finger and stick into pig for a tail. Press on eyes. Using a pencil, make grooves for eyebrows.
3. Paint pig when dry.

60

Treasure in Heaven

Jewelry Box

Mark 10:21

Per Child Supplies

Small cardboard box with lid
Many small twigs no bigger than a pencil
Shells, beads, dried flowers, or small pinecones
Felt or velvet
Scripture on small placard
String

Instructions

1. Glue Scripture placard to center of box lid. Frame by covering entire box lid with creatively organized twigs and ornaments (shells, beads, flowers, or pinecones) until lid is covered.
2. Using twigs, cover the lower portion of the box by aligning twigs vertically around perimeter. Glue in place, using string to keep in place until dry.
3. Press velvet or felt inside box to line. Attach with glue or staples.

61

The Widow's Mite

Wall Hanging

Mark 12:42

Per Child Supplies

Self-drying clay

Large paper clip

1 quarter

Long, thin strip on which the Scripture is written

Shellac or mixture of 2/3 glue, 1/3 water

Instructions

1. Form the clay into a long, flat oval. Press opened paper clip into back to form hanger.
2. On the front, press quarter into center. Use a pencil to make creative etchings alongside quarter, such as leaves, birds, etc.
3. When almost dry, paint. When paint is dry, glue on Scripture and coat entire project with shellac or glue-water mixture.

MARK
12:42

But a poor
widow came
and put a
. . .

62

Watching and Praying

Pretend Clock

Mark 14:38

Per Child Supplies

2 black construction-paper clock hands
1 brass brad
Piece of cardboard
Construction paper
Assortment of small dried or pressed flowers, seeds, or leaves

Instructions

1. Glue construction paper to cardboard. Punch hole in center. Affix hands with brad.
2. Write numbers *12, 3, 6,* and *9* on clock. For other numbers, glue on a seed, flower, etc. Write on the clock face "ANYTIME IS A GOOD TIME TO PRAY."

139

63

Live by the Spirit

Wall Hanging

Galatians 5:16

Per Child Supplies

Fir or palm fronds
Washable, nontoxic paint
Large washbasin and access to water and soap
12-inch cardboard circle with holes punched into it
Yarn
Scripture
2 6-inch construction paper semicircles to cover cardboard

Instructions

1. Glue semicircles to cardboard. Mark holes by impressing with finger or pencil tip.
2. Remove socks and shoes. Pour paint into washbasin to 1/8-inch depth. Step in with both feet, and immediately step onto circle. Wash feet.
3. When footprints are dry, glue on Scripture. Affix fir or palm fronds with yarn, using holes. Make a yarn hanger through the top hole.

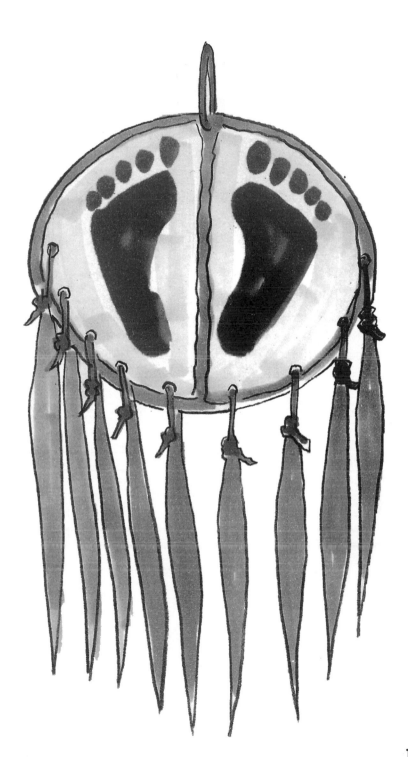

A Pleasing Aroma

Potpourri Sachet

Philippians 4:18

Per Child Supplies

1 calico circle with pinked edges, 6–8 inches in diameter
Scripture on small tagboard card with hole punched in corner
8–12 cotton balls
Rose or sandalwood potpourri oil
Collection of dried small flower petals, seeds, foliage
Rubber band
Ribbon

Instructions

1. In nonmetallic bowl, mix all flora with oil, like a salad. Put a few drops of oil on cotton balls.
2. Place cotton balls and flora in center of cloth. Bind with rubber band to form a ball.
3. Run ribbon through hole in Scripture card, then tie neck with ribbon.

65

Faith Defined

Mosaic

Hebrews 11:1

Per Child Supplies

Broken eggshells, dyed in primary colors
Piece of small oval cardboard
Scripture in calligraphy on beige paper
1/2-inch ruffled lace
Yarn for hanger

Instructions

1. Glue Scripture to center of oval. Glue eggshells in any pattern around oval to the edges. It is possible to use care and create detailed pictures in mosaic, but not all children will be able to do this.
2. Carefully glue lace to the back of the cardboard, seamed side against backing. Glue on yarn hanger.

Comments

Project can be coated with shellac, a mixture of 2/3 glue, 1/3 water, or thinned gold paint when it is completed.

Now faith is being sure of what we hope for and certain of what we do not see.

HEBREWS 11:1

Prayers for the Sick

Prayer List

James 5:15

Per Child Supplies

1 5 x 7 inch ruled notepad

Weathered wooden board larger than the pad

Assorted dried weeds and flowers on stems, pieces of bark, lichen, etc.

8 brass finishing nails

7 x 2 inch piece of suede or rawhide

Pencil

Piece of jute

Instructions

1. Arrange top flowers and nail the notepad to the board with two nails, trapping the stems.
2. Cut suede or rawhide in half—two 7 x 1 inch pieces. Cut one piece in half again—3 1/2 x 1 inch.
3. Across larger piece of suede write "_____'S PRAYER LIST" (using the child's name). Cover the top of the pad with the suede. Nail in place.
4. On each side of notepad, arrange vegetation, cover ends with suede, and use taut pressure while nailing to wood. Use glue if too brittle. For one nail, tie a knot in the end of the jute; nail through knot, through suede, and into wood. Tie pencil to other end of jute.

67

The Grass Withers

Miniature Garden

1 Peter 1:24

Per Child Supplies

Disposable aluminum pie tin
1/4 cup grass seed
Mesh netting (like potatoes come in)
Black book-shaped cutout, 2 inches wide
White pages with Scripture written on them for inside book

Instructions

1. Put grass seed in tin. Cover tin with netting and tie or staple in place.
2. Glue white pages to black book. Glue book to netting in center of pie tin.
3. Add a small amount of water to sprout the seeds so they are *damp*, not floating. Keep damp.

68

Living Stones

Model

1 Peter 2:5

Per Child Supplies

Collection of child's-palm-sized stones or rocks
Pipe cleaners
Construction paper
Bits of lace and fabric
Paint
Yarn

Instructions

1. Wash rocks thoroughly.
2. Decorate by making yarn wigs, painting on faces, making construction paper hats and clothes, and designing ties and necklines from lace and fabric. Use pipe cleaners to create weird hairstyles, to form ties, arms, and legs.

Comments

This craft requires almost no preparation, encourages creativity and use of natural resources, and exemplifies an important Scripture. One might choose to remind young students of the power God must have to be able to really make rocks into people.

Autumn Leaves

Sun Catcher

Jude 12

Per Child Supplies

2 pieces cardboard, 8-inches diameter
2 pieces plastic wrap
Assorted felt or dried leaves
Lace or trim
Yarn for hanger

Instructions

1. Cut cardboard into circles and fold in half. Cut out center, leaving a 2-inch margin.
2. Glue one piece of plastic wrap to one piece of cardboard. (It will not stick well yet.) Glue leaves to margin so they cover the opening of the cardboard. Glue second piece of plastic wrap to leaves. Glue on yarn for hanger.
3. Put a thin line of glue around perimeter of circle. Repeat 1/4 inch in. On outer circle of glue, press on lace or trim (ruffle out, seam side in). Press other sheet of cardboard down.
4. Hold in place with paper clips until dry. While it is drying, glue leaves to front to cover cardboard. Scripture may be added.

Scripture Index

Numbers in lightfaced type refer to Project Number

Age Index

Numbers in lightfaced type refer to Project Number

All ages	8
3 & up	1, 2, 21, 25, 32, 40, 52, 53, 57, 61, 63, 64
3–6	4, 10, 27, 67
3–9	13, 18, 29, 30, 34, 38, 44, 62, 68
6 & up	3, 11, 19, 22, 23, 26, 31, 35, 36, 37, 39, 41, 45, 46, 47, 48, 50, 51, 54, 55, 59, 66, 69
6–9	6, 14, 49
9 & up	9, 12, 15, 16, 17, 20, 24, 28, 33, 42, 43, 56, 58, 60, 65
9–12	5, 7